United States Government Accountability Office

Report to Congressional Committees

I0448166

July 2013

SEC CONFLICT MINERALS RULE

Information on Responsible Sourcing and Companies Affected

GAO Highlights

Highlights of GAO-13-689, a report to congressional committees

SEC CONFLICT MINERALS RULE

Information on Responsible Sourcing and Companies Affected

Why GAO Did This Study

The eastern part of the DRC has experienced recurring conflicts involving armed groups that have resulted in severe human rights abuses. In addition, armed groups have profited from the exploitation of minerals. In 2010, Congress enacted Section 1502(b) of the Dodd-Frank Wall Street Reform and Consumer Protection Act to address the exploitation of conflict minerals, which include tin, tantalum, tungsten, and gold, and the extreme levels of violence in the DRC. As required by Section 1502(b), the SEC issued a rule in August 2012 that requires companies to disclose their use of conflict minerals and the origin of those minerals. The act requires GAO to report on the rule's effectiveness, among other issues, beginning in 2012 and annually thereafter.

Initial company disclosure reports to SEC that would enable GAO to assess the effectiveness of the rule will not be due until May 2014. This report describes, among other issues, (1) factors that may impact whether SEC's rule denies armed groups in the DRC benefits from conflict minerals and (2) information about companies that use conflict minerals and are not required to report to SEC under the rule.

GAO reviewed and analyzed documents and interviewed representatives from SEC, the Department of State, the U.S. Agency for International Development, industry associations, NGOs, consulting firms, and international organizations. GAO also analyzed smelter and refiner information. This report does not contain recommendations.

View GAO-13-689. For more information, contact Lawrance L. Evans, Jr. at (202) 512-4802 or evansl@gao.gov.

What GAO Found

Stakeholder-developed initiatives may facilitate companies' compliance with the Securities and Exchange Commission's (SEC) final conflict minerals rule, but other factors may affect the rule's impact on reducing benefits to armed groups in the Democratic Republic of the Congo (DRC) and neighboring countries. Agency and industry officials as well as representatives from international organizations and nongovernmental organizations (NGO) stated that adoption of the rule as well as stakeholder-developed initiatives—which include the development of guidance documents, audit protocols, and in-region sourcing of conflict minerals—can support companies' efforts to conduct due diligence and to identify and responsibly source conflict minerals. For example, officials GAO interviewed explained that the Conflict-Free Smelter Program enables suppliers to source conflict minerals from smelters (companies that refine the ore of the conflict minerals into metals) that have been certified by an independent third-party auditor as obtaining their minerals from sources that did not benefit armed groups. However, officials GAO interviewed cited constraining factors such as lack of security, lack of infrastructure, and lack of capacity in the DRC that could affect the ability to expand on efforts to achieve conflict-free sourcing of minerals from eastern DRC and thereby potentially contribute to armed groups' benefiting from the conflict minerals trade. For example, officials GAO interviewed noted that there is a lack of infrastructure in place that would enable companies to set up or expand operations in the DRC. Limited transportation and poor roads in eastern DRC also make it difficult to get to mine sites. Moreover, according to officials, the remoteness of mines also makes it difficult for DRC officials to validate mines and ensure that the mines have not been compromised by illegal armed groups.

Companies that are not required to file disclosures under SEC's conflict minerals rule may be affected by the rule. These companies may supply components or parts that contain conflict minerals to companies that report to SEC under the rule, many of which could be original equipment manufacturers and component parts manufacturers. Estimates provided by public commentators responding to the rule indicate that roughly 280,000 suppliers could provide products to roughly 6,000 companies that report to the SEC under the rule and may be asked to provide information on their use of conflict minerals and the origin of the minerals as part of the rule's due diligence requirements. GAO found little available aggregated information about companies that do not report to SEC under the rule. However, GAO found that for smelters and refiners there is some aggregated information, such as the types of conflict minerals they use and their location. For example, GAO found that over half of the 278 smelters and refiners of conflict minerals it identified were located in Asia, many processed tin, and most did not have a conflict minerals policy publicly available.

Contents

Letter		1
	Background	4
	Stakeholder-Developed Initiatives May Facilitate Compliance with Conflict Minerals Rule, but Other Factors May Affect the Rule's Impact on Reducing Benefits to Armed Groups	12
	Many Companies Not Required to Report to SEC under the Conflict Minerals Rule Will Likely Be Affected; Limited Aggregated Information about Them Exists	20
	Little Additional Information on the Rate of Sexual Violence in Eastern DRC and Neighboring Countries Has Become Available since GAO's 2012 Report	31
	Agency Comments and Our Evaluation	34

Appendix I	Objectives, Scope, and Methodology	37

Appendix II	SEC's Flowchart Summary of the Disclosure Process for the Final Conflict Minerals Rule	41

Appendix III	Updates of Global and In-Region Sourcing Initiatives	43
	Global Sourcing Initiatives	43
	In-Region Sourcing Initiatives	45

Appendix IV	GAO Contacts and Staff Acknowledgments	47

Figures

Figure 1: Map of DRC with Provinces and Neighboring Countries	5
Figure 2: Timeline for SEC-Reporting Companies to Submit Conflict Minerals Disclosures to SEC	9
Figure 3: Simplified Conflict Minerals Supply Chain	11
Figure 4: Simplified Conflict Minerals Supply Chain Showing Supplier Tiers	23
Figure 5: Flow of Supply Chain Inquiries from the Original Equipment Manufacturers to the Mine	24
Figure 6: Number of Smelters and Refiners of Conflict Minerals We Identified, by Country	28
Figure 7: Population-Based Surveys That Estimate the Rate of Sexual Violence in Eastern DRC, Rwanda, and Uganda	32
Figure 8: SEC's Flowchart Summary of the Final Conflict Minerals Rule	42

Abbreviations

DHS	Demographic and Health Survey
Dodd-Frank Act	Dodd-Frank Wall Street Reform and Consumer Protection Act
DRC	Democratic Republic of the Congo
EICC	Electronic Industry Citizenship Coalition
GeSI	Global e-Sustainability Initiative
ICGLR	International Conference of the Great Lakes Region
iTSCi	ITRI Tin Supply Chain Initiative
LBMA	London Bullion Market Association
M23	March 23 Movement
MONUSCO	United Nations Organization Stabilization Mission in the Democratic Republic of the Congo
NGO	nongovernmental organization
OECD	Organisation for Economic Co-operation and Development
PPA	Public-Private Alliance for Responsible Minerals Trade
SEC	Securities and Exchange Commission
State	United States Department of State
UN	United Nations
UNGoE	United Nations Group of Experts
USAID	United States Agency for International Development

July 18, 2013

Congressional Committees

The Democratic Republic of the Congo (DRC) has long been the site of one of the world's worst humanitarian crises. Since 1998, over 5.4 million people have died as a result of the conflict which has also destabilized the eastern part of the country, created insecurity, displaced people, and perpetuated the cycle of poverty, according to estimates by the International Rescue Committee. In 2010 we reported that illegal armed groups, as well as some units of the Congolese national military, had continued to commit severe human rights abuses, including mass killings.[1] In 2013 the United Nations (UN) reported continuing violence by illegal armed groups, including violence by the group known as M23.[2] Sexual violence has also been a feature of the conflict in the DRC at least since the Congolese civil war of the mid-1990s. The illegal armed groups and units of the Congolese national military committing these atrocities also profit from the illegal mining of minerals. In response to the humanitarian situation in the DRC, Congress included in the Dodd-Frank Wall Street Reform and Consumer Protection Act (hereafter referred to as the Dodd-Frank Act, or the Act) provisions pertaining to the trade of DRC conflict minerals—tantalum, tin, tungsten, and gold.[3] Specifically, section 1502(a) of the Act states that "It is the sense of the Congress that the exploitation and trade of conflict minerals originating in the [DRC] is helping to finance conflict characterized by extreme levels of violence in the eastern [DRC], particularly sexual- and gender-based violence, and contributing to an emergency humanitarian situation therein." Section 1502(b) of the Act required the Securities and Exchange Commission (SEC) to issue a conflict minerals disclosure rule that requires issuers

---

[1]GAO, *The Democratic Republic of the Congo: U.S. Agencies Should Take Further Actions to Contribute to the Effective Regulation and Control of the Minerals Trade in Eastern Democratic Republic of the Congo*, GAO-10-1030 (Washington, D.C.: Sept. 30, 2010).

[2]According to the UN, M23, for March 23 Movement, is an armed group that formed in May 2012 in eastern DRC.

[3]The Dodd-Frank Act defines conflict minerals as columbite-tantalite (coltan), cassiterite, gold, wolframite, or their derivatives, and any other mineral or its derivatives determined by the Secretary of State. Columbite-tantalite (coltan), cassiterite, and wolframite ores are ores from which tantalum, tin, and tungsten, respectively, are processed.

with conflict minerals that are necessary to the functionality or production of a product manufactured by such persons to file reports annually with SEC to disclose whether any of those minerals originated in the DRC or an adjoining country, and if so, to provide an additional report.[4] In response to section 1502 of the Act, SEC adopted the final conflict minerals rule on August 22, 2012.[5] The Act also required us to report, beginning in 2012 and annually thereafter, on the effectiveness of the rule in promoting peace and security in the DRC and adjoining countries; to describe information that may be publicly available about entities that use conflict minerals but are not required to report to SEC under the rule; and report, annually beginning in 2011, on the rate of sexual violence in war-torn areas of the DRC and neighboring countries. To address the mandate, in July 2011 we issued our first report on sexual violence[6] and in July 2012 we issued our second report, which focused on SEC's actions and stakeholder-developed initiatives involving conflict minerals and updated information on the rate of sexual violence.[7]

As in our 2012 report, we did not address the effectiveness of SEC's conflict minerals disclosure rule, as required under the legislation, because the first disclosures of companies' use of conflict minerals will not be due to SEC until May 2014 and sufficient time must elapse to allow the full impact of the rule to materialize. However, the effectiveness of the rule in promoting peace and security in the DRC will depend in part on its ability to limit funding by restricting the use of conflict minerals to illegal armed groups in the region to which those groups have access. As a result, this report describes (1) factors that may impact whether SEC's conflict minerals rule denies armed groups in the DRC and adjoining countries benefits from conflict minerals; (2) available information about entities that use conflict minerals and are not required to report to SEC

---

[4]The countries adjoining the DRC are Angola, Zambia, Tanzania, Burundi, Rwanda, Uganda, South Sudan, Central African Republic, and the Republic of the Congo.

[5]77 Federal Register at 56274 (Sept. 12, 2012).

[6]GAO, *The Democratic Republic of the Congo: Information on the Rate of Sexual Violence in War-Torn Eastern DRC and Adjoining Countries*, GAO-11-702 (Washington, D.C.: July 13, 2011).

[7]GAO, *Conflict Minerals Disclosure Rule: SEC's Actions and Stakeholder-Developed Initiatives*, GAO-12-763 (Washington, D.C.: July 16, 2012). In the report, we addressed the mandate requiring us to descr be any issues that SEC encountered in promulgating a conflict minerals disclosure rule.

under the rule;[8] and (3) any additional information available on the rate of sexual violence in eastern DRC and neighboring countries since our 2012 report.[9]

To address these objectives, we reviewed and analyzed reports and other documents from relevant U.S. agencies; multilateral organizations, such as the Organisation for Economic Co-operation and Development (OECD); nongovernmental organizations (NGO); and industry associations. We also analyzed information on tin, tantalum, tungsten, and gold smelters and refiners to ascertain the location of these entities as well as whether they had posted any conflict-free sourcing policies on their companies' websites. We interviewed officials, who are cognizant of conflict minerals issues, from SEC, the Department of State (State), and the United States Agency for International Development (USAID), as well as representatives from international organizations, NGOs, industry associations, consulting firms, and smelters and refiners of tin, tantalum, tungsten, and gold.[10] We chose the experts and stakeholders we interviewed to capture a range of perspectives about the types of minerals traded and because we had established contacts with these entities on our last review. These experts and stakeholders constitute a nongeneralizable sample. The information gathered cannot be generalized and cannot be used to infer views of other experts or stakeholders cognizant of conflict minerals issues. In the interviews, we asked the experts and stakeholders to provide factors that they believe may impact whether SEC's conflict minerals rule denies armed groups in the DRC benefits from conflict minerals. We identified 278 smelters and refiners of tin, tantalum, tungsten, and gold, and analyzed publicly available information on their practices and policies for sourcing conflict minerals, including any due diligence guidance the smelters or refiners reportedly followed for sourcing conflict minerals. We identified 278 smelters and refiners in our analysis; the total number of smelters and

---

[8]We did not have access to information about specific entities or companies so we described what we learned about entities that are not required to report to the SEC under the conflict minerals rule.

[9]As we reported in 2012, the neighboring countries of eastern DRC are Burundi, Rwanda, and Uganda.

[10]For our review, we selected smelters to interview based on the types of minerals the smelters processed and their willingness to speak with us. We sought to speak with officials of at least one smelter or refiner for each of the conflict minerals—tin, tantalum, tungsten, and gold.

GAO-13-689 SEC Conflict Minerals Rule

refiners is believed to be nearly 500, worldwide. The number of gold refiners could potentially be larger, considering that little equipment and space is required to refine gold, and it can be refined at the mine site. The 278 smelters and refiners we were able to identify may not be representative of others, and the information we report about these 278 cannot be generalized to other smelters and refiners of tin, tantalum, tungsten, and gold. See appendix I for a complete description of our scope and methodology.

We conducted this performance audit from November 2012 to July 2013 in accordance with generally accepted government auditing standards. Those standards require that we plan and perform the audit to obtain sufficient, appropriate evidence to provide a reasonable basis for our findings and conclusions based on our audit objectives. We believe that the evidence obtained provides a reasonable basis for our findings and conclusions based on our audit objectives.

Background

History of the DRC: Conflict and Instability

The mineral-rich DRC, Africa's second-largest country, has been plagued by cycles of violence and instability. Since 1998, violent conflicts, poverty, and disease have killed more than 5.4 million people in the country, according to estimates by the International Rescue Committee. The DRC was colonized as a personal possession of Belgian King Leopold II in 1885 and administered by the Belgian government starting in 1907. It achieved independence from Belgium in 1960. For almost 30 years of the post-independence period, the DRC, then known as Zaire, was ruled by an authoritarian regime under Mobutu Sese Seko. Following the 1994 genocide in Rwanda and the establishment of a new government there, some perpetrators of the genocide and refugees fled to the neighboring Kivu provinces of eastern DRC. A rebellion began there in 1996, pitting the forces led by Laurent Kabila against the army of President Mobutu Sese Seko. Kabila's forces, aided by Rwanda and Uganda, took the capital city of Kinshasa in 1997 and renamed the country the Democratic Republic of the Congo. See figure 1 for a map of the DRC's provinces and neighboring countries.

Figure 1: Map of DRC with Provinces and Neighboring Countries

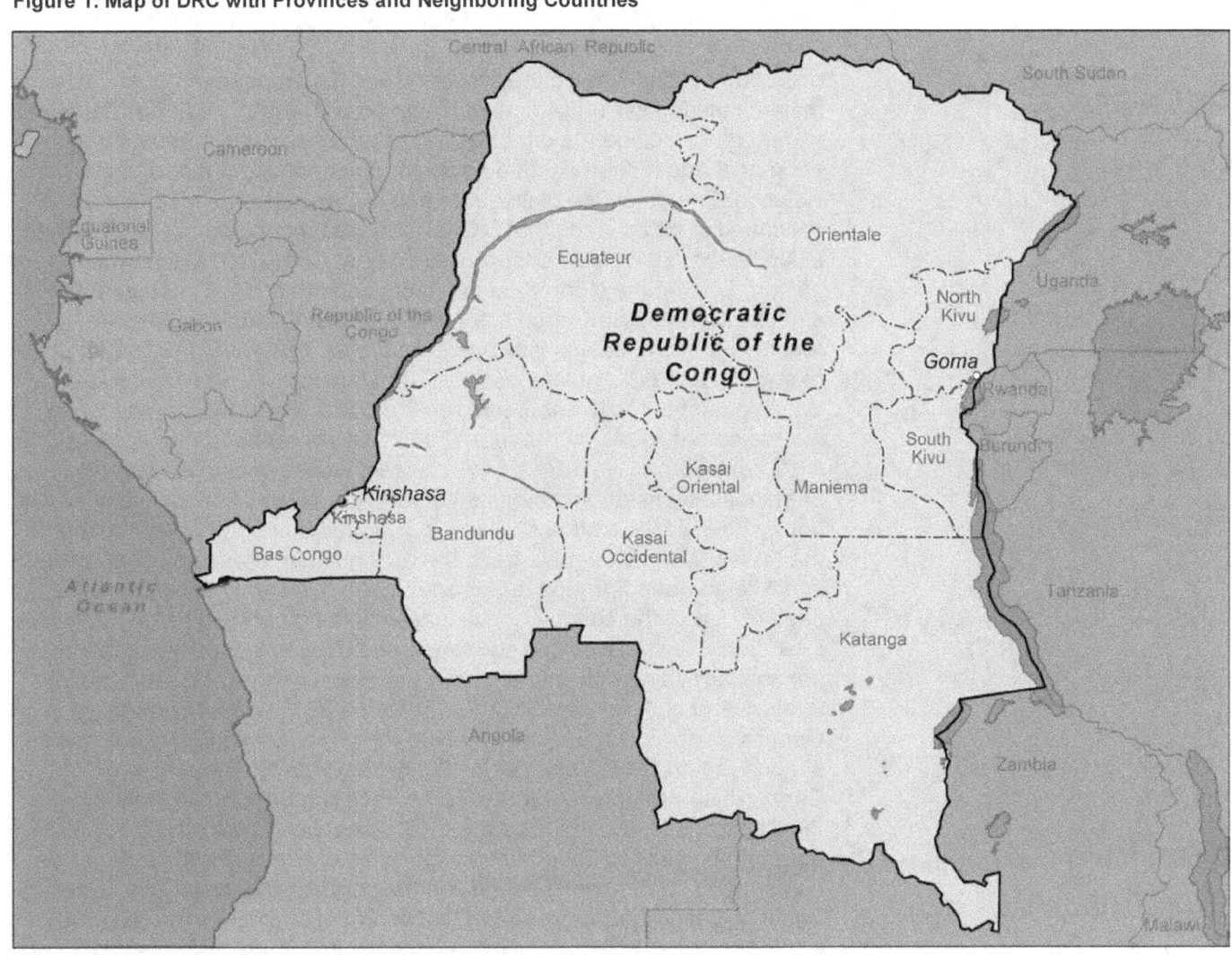

Source: GAO; United Nations (map).

A period of civil war among rival rebel groups ensued. In 2001 Laurent Kabila was assassinated and leadership shifted to his son Joseph Kabila, while the civil war continued. Starting in 1999 the UN Security Council

GAO-13-689 SEC Conflict Minerals Rule

authorized peacekeeping operations in the DRC which have been operating as the United Nations Organization Stabilization Mission in the Democratic Republic of the Congo (MONUSCO).[11] Initially, the operation's focus was on the ceasefire and disengagement of forces and maintenance of liaison with all parties involved with the civil war but then expanded to include the effective protection of civilians, humanitarian personnel and human rights defenders under imminent threat of physical violence. The presence of illegal armed groups, such as M23, has continued to be an issue that MONUSCO has monitored in recent years. In November 2012, M23 occupied the city of Goma, a provincial capital in eastern DRC in the North Kivu province, and other cities in eastern DRC and clashed with the Congolese national army. During this time, the UN reported cases of sexual violence perpetrated by armed groups and members of the Congolese national army against women and children. While M23 eventually withdrew from the cities, the group's presence in the region continues. In February 2013, the UN reported that eastern DRC continues to be plagued by recurrent waves of conflict, chronic humanitarian crises, and serious human rights violations, including sexual and gender-based violence. The report added that contributing factors to the cycles of violence have been the continuing presence of Congolese and foreign armed groups taking advantage of security vacuums in the eastern part of the country, the illegal exploitation of resources, interference by neighboring countries, and the weak capacity of the national army and police to effectively protect civilians and the national territory and ensure law and order. In March 2013, the UN Secretary-General appointed a Special Envoy to the Great Lakes Region of Africa to support the implementation of the 11-nation "Peace, Security and Cooperation Framework for the Democratic Republic of the Congo and the Region" adopted in February 2013. According to the UN, the agreement seeks to end the recurring cycle of conflicts and crisis in the eastern DRC and to build peace. Additionally, on March 28, 2013, the UN Security Council authorized the deployment of an intervention brigade within the current peacekeeping operations in DRC to address imminent threats to peace and security. The objectives of the new force based in North Kivu province are to neutralize armed groups, reduce the threat they pose to state authority and civilian security, and make space for stabilization activities.

---

[11]MONUSCO took over from an earlier UN peacekeeping operation—the United Nations Organization Mission in Democratic Republic of the Congo—on July 1, 2010.

U.S. Government Response to Situation in the DRC	Congress has focused on issues related to the DRC for almost a decade. In 2006, Congress passed the Democratic Republic of Congo Relief, Security, and Democracy Promotion Act of 2006.[12] The act stated that it is the policy of the United States, among other things, to engage with governments working for peace and security throughout the DRC and hold accountable individuals, entities, and countries working to destabilize the government. In July 2010, Congress included several provisions in section 1502 of the Dodd-Frank Act related to conflict minerals in the DRC and adjoining countries.[13] Specifically, section 1502(a) of the Act states that "it is the sense of Congress that the exploitation and trade of conflict minerals originating in the [DRC] is helping to finance conflict characterized by extreme levels of violence in the eastern Democratic Republic of the Congo, particularly sexual- and gender-based violence, and contributing to an emergency humanitarian situation therein," warranting the provisions of Section 1502(b) of the Act. Section 1502(b) requires SEC, in consultation with State, to promulgate disclosure and reporting regulations regarding the use of conflict minerals from the DRC and adjoining countries. In November 2011, State and USAID, in collaboration with NGOs, industry, and other governments, launched the Public-Private Alliance for Responsible Minerals Trade (PPA) to support responsible supply chain solutions regarding conflict minerals from the DRC and neighboring countries. The PPA supports pilot programs, with the ultimate goal of producing scalable, self-sustaining systems, to demonstrate a fully traced and validated conflict-mineral supply chain in a way that is credible to companies, civil society, and government. According to USAID, in addition to the PPA, the U.S. government's contribution to the Responsible Minerals Trade Program in the DRC region has amounted to almost $19 million and includes activities focused on the protection of artisanal mining communities, institutional and human capacity building for responsible minerals trade, and capacity building in mining sector security, among other issues.

---

[12]Pub. L. No. 109-456, sec 102(14).

[13]Pub. L. No.111-203, sec 1502. According to an expert in conflict minerals that we interviewed, Canada and the European Union have taken steps to propose conflict minerals initiatives: Canada has a proposed conflict minerals rule that is currently in its comment period, and the European Union currently is having consultations on a potential conflicts minerals rule.

SEC's Final Conflict Minerals Rule

The SEC Commissioners adopted[14] the final conflict minerals rule on August 22, 2012, after a number of delays during the drafting process.[15] SEC reported that during its rule-making process it received more than 400 letters commenting on the draft rule.[16] As adopted, the final rule applies to any issuer that files reports with SEC under Section 13(a) or Section 15(d) of the Securities Exchange Act of 1934[17] (Securities Exchange Act) and uses conflict minerals that are necessary to the functionality or production of a product manufactured or contracted by that issuer to be manufactured. According to SEC, issuers that have a reporting obligation are domestic and foreign companies that offer shares publicly and file forms 10-K, 20-F, or 40-F with SEC. For the purposes of our report, we refer to those issuing companies affected by the rule as "SEC-reporting companies under the rule." (See app. II for more information on the steps a company needs to take to fulfill its reporting requirements.) Under the rule, such companies must file a disclosure report and conduct a "reasonable country of origin inquiry" to determine whether they must also file a conflict minerals report.[18] Companies that are required to file a conflict minerals report must exercise due diligence on the source and chain of custody of their conflict minerals. The due diligence measures used by companies must conform to a nationally or internationally recognized due diligence framework, such as the due diligence guidance approved by OECD. If a company determines that its products are "DRC conflict-free" because they may have originated from the covered countries but did not finance or benefit armed groups, then the company must obtain an independent private sector audit and provide certification that it conducted an audit. If a company's products have not been found to be "DRC conflict-free," then the company must provide additional information in its conflict minerals report. For a temporary period—4 years for smaller reporting companies or 2 years for all other

---

[14]According to SEC, when SEC proposes or adopts a set of rules, often those rules are contained in a single document, called a proposing release or adopting release.

[15]In 2012 we reported on some of the factors that caused delays in developing, modifying, and finalizing the rule. GAO-12-763.

[16]SEC reported that commentary came from corporations, professional associations, human rights and public policy groups, bar associations, auditors, institutional investors, investment firms, U.S. and foreign government officials, consumers, and other interested parties and stakeholders.

[17]15 U.S.C. § 78m(a) and 78o(d).

[18]According to SEC, the report will be filed on Form SD.

reporting companies—if a company is unable to determine whether the minerals in its products originated in the DRC or the adjoining countries or financed or benefited armed groups in those countries, then those products are considered "DRC conflict undeterminable" and no audit is required.[19] Under the rule, all companies will need to file their first disclosure report to SEC on May 31, 2014, which covers the 2013 calendar year, and on May 31 annually thereafter. Figure 2 shows the reporting time frames for SEC-reporting companies under the rule.

Figure 2: Timeline for SEC-Reporting Companies to Submit Conflict Minerals Disclosures to SEC

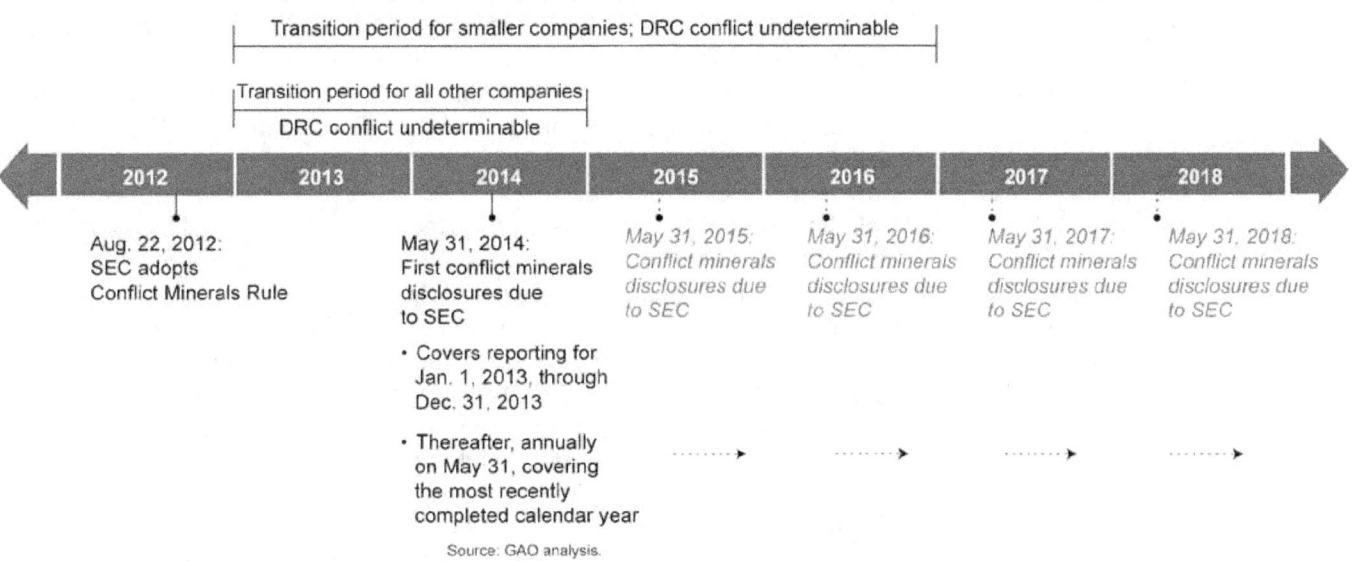

Source: GAO analysis.

---

[19]According to the SEC rule, SEC-reporting companies may describe their products as "DRC conflict undeterminable" if, following their exercise of due diligence, they are unable to determine that their minerals meet the statutory definition of "DRC conflict-free" because they have conflict minerals from the DRC or the adjoining countries but were unable to determine if their conflict minerals financed or benefited armed groups; or they had reason to believe that their conflict minerals may have originated in the DRC and adjoining countries and may not have come from recycled or scrap sources and the information gathered failed to clarify the conflict minerals' country of origin, benefits to armed groups, or whether it came from scrap or recycled sources.

In October 2012, the U.S. Chamber of Commerce, the National Association of Manufacturers, and the Business Roundtable filed a lawsuit against SEC regarding the final conflict minerals rule.[20] In their petition, the two industry associations asked that the rule "be modified or set aside in whole or in part." The petitioners have asked the court to review, among other things, whether SEC's economic analysis is inadequate and whether SEC's interpretations of certain key terms in section 1502 of the Act are consistent with congressional intent.

Conflict Minerals Description and Supply Chain

The four conflict minerals covered by section 1502(b) of the Dodd-Frank Act are mined in various locations around the world. For example, tin is predominantly mined in China, Indonesia, Peru, and Bolivia, as well as in the DRC, while tantalum is reportedly predominantly mined in areas such as Australia, Brazil, and Canada. From 2006 through 2011, the majority of tungsten production—reportedly 77 to 87 percent of global production—was mined in China. Gold, however, is mined in many different countries, including the DRC. Our review of United States Geological Survey data on tantalum, tin, tungsten, and gold mined in the DRC showed that about 12 percent of the global tantalum supply and less than 1 percent of the global tungsten supply was mined in the DRC in 2011. About 3 percent of the global tin supply, and less than 1 percent of the global gold supply, was mined in the DRC in 2010. As we reported in our 2012 report, various industries, particularly in manufacturing, use these minerals in a wide variety of products and in varying amounts. For example, many industries use tin in the form of tin solder, which is used to join metal pieces together.[21] According to company representatives, tin is also found in food packaging, in steel coatings on automobile parts, and in some plastics. According to industry association and company representatives, the majority of tantalum is used to manufacture tantalum capacitors, which enable energy storage in electronic products such as cell phones

---

[20]National Association of Manufacturers, Chamber of Commerce of the United States of America, and Business Roundtable v. U.S. Securities and Exchange Commission, 12-1422, U.S. Court of Appeals for the District of Columbia Circuit. In May 2013, the U.S. Court of Appeals transferred the case to the U.S. District Court for the District of Columbia citing a recent jurisdictional decision based on a similar case.

[21]See GAO-12-763. For example, tin solder is used to attach individual components on circuit boards.

GAO-13-689 SEC Conflict Minerals Rule

and computers.[22] Tungsten is used in automobile manufacturing, drill bits and cutting tools, and other industrial manufacturing tools. It is also the primary component of filaments in light bulbs. In addition to its use as currency and in jewelry, gold is also used by other industries, such as the electronics industry.

A company's supply chain for products containing tin, tantalum, tungsten, and gold can be complex and can vary considerably in the way it operates, according to industry association and company representatives. Generally, however, the supply chain for companies using conflict minerals begins at the mine site, where tin, tantalum, and tungsten ore are extracted from the ground using mechanized or artisanal mining techniques.[23] Figure 3 provides additional information on a simplified supply chain for all four conflict minerals.

Figure 3: Simplified Conflict Minerals Supply Chain

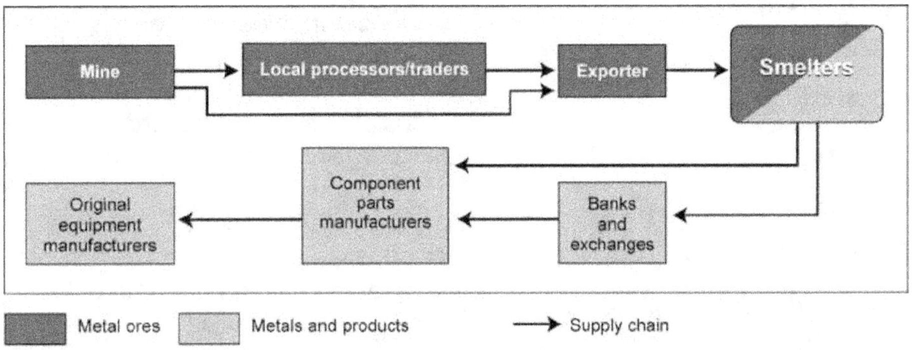

Source: GAO analysis.

For artisanal mining, the local processor or trader (which may be an individual or company) purchases minerals directly from the mine sites and typically processes or upgrades them before selling them to an exporter. The exporter may also purchase minerals directly from mine

---

[22]Tantalum is also used to produce alloy additives, which can be found in turbines in jet engines; mill and chemical products; thin films, which are used in semiconductors; and other products.

[23]Artisanal mining is a form of mining that is characterized by a lack of mechanization or capital investment.

sites rather than going through a local processor or trader. Exporters may carry out further processing or upgrading before exporting materials to a smelter or refiner, where they are either converted into metals or purified into a higher-purity metal. Smelters primarily provide high-purity tin, tantalum, and tungsten directly to component parts manufacturers, although some sell high-purity metals through traders or exchanges.[24] Gold refiners typically sell high-purity gold to banks, for use as a store of value, or to international exchanges, where gold is bought and sold.[25] However, some gold refiners sell gold directly to manufacturers as well. Banks and traders may sell gold to manufacturers, including jewelry and component parts manufacturers. The component parts manufacturers construct individual parts—such as capacitors, engine parts, or clasps for necklaces—that they sell to original equipment manufacturers. The original equipment manufacturers complete the final assembly of a product and sell the final product to the consumer.

Stakeholder-Developed Initiatives May Facilitate Compliance with Conflict Minerals Rule, but Other Factors May Affect the Rule's Impact on Reducing Benefits to Armed Groups

SEC's adoption of the final conflict minerals rule on August 22, 2012, has raised companies' awareness regarding conflict minerals and the due diligence necessary to identify whether conflict minerals may have benefited armed groups. Specifically, officials representing industry associations stated that the final conflict minerals rule has acted as an impetus for some of their members to start thinking about whether the rule impacts them and some have also started collecting information to comply with the rule. Officials stated that stakeholder-developed initiatives, such as in-region and global sourcing initiatives, may increase companies' assurance that conflict minerals they are using are not benefiting armed groups in the DRC and neighboring countries. However, constraining factors such as the lack of security, lack of infrastructure, and capacity constraints could undermine companies' ability to ensure conflict-free sourcing from the region.

---

[24]According to OECD, in many instances smelters and refiners do not actually take ownership of the mineral but provide a service and charge a fee based on the amount of minerals smelted. Ownership of the minerals may remain with the mineral trader, bank, or component parts manufacturer.

[25]According to a World Gold Council representative, in most cases refiners are paid a fee to refine gold and the transaction is conducted between the miner, trader, and the bank.

Adoption of the Final Rule Has Raised Companies' Awareness Regarding Sourcing of Conflict Minerals

Since SEC issued the final conflict minerals rule pursuant to the Dodd Frank Act, companies have become more aware of the issues surrounding conflict minerals and have started to consider the source of materials used in products, given the requirement in the final rule for a company that uses tin, tantalum, tungsten, or gold to exercise due diligence on the source and chain of custody of its conflict minerals, if there is reason to believe that they may have originated in the DRC or an adjoining country.[26] According to some industry officials we interviewed, the final rule has helped resolve some uncertainties, such as the breadth of the industries covered, that existed before the promulgation of the rule. Numerous industry officials and representatives from international organizations and NGOs we interviewed have indicated that the creation and promulgation of the SEC rule has increased visibility into the issue of conflict minerals and raised awareness of the due diligence process, particularly for those companies that are not required to report under the rule but that may still be impacted indirectly by the rule.[27] Specifically, officials of industry associations representing member companies that use tin, tantalum, tungsten, or gold in their products stated that many companies are aware of the SEC rule, especially the larger companies that may file a disclosure report with SEC, and are working to start complying with the rule. Some smaller companies, which may not be required to report under the rule, may not be as aware of or familiar with the rule but are receiving information from industry associations on how the rule may impact them. For example, some officials from industry associations stated that they were putting together guidance documents that break down the SEC rule and had also sent questions to SEC seeking to clarify points in the rule. Agency officials stated that the SEC rule has raised visibility globally of conflict minerals. For example, State reported in February 2013 that the issuance of the SEC rule was a vital step in establishing a clear and harmonized global framework for responsible minerals trade from the DRC region. Furthermore, State

---

[26]OECD defines "due diligence" as an ongoing, proactive, and reactive process through which companies can ensure that they respect human rights and do not contribute to conflict. Due diligence can also help companies ensure that they observe international law and comply with domestic laws, including those governing the illicit trade in minerals and UN sanctions. Risk-based due diligence refers to the steps companies should take to identify and address actual or potential risks in order to prevent or mitigate adverse impacts associated with their activities or sourcing decisions.

[27]Some agency officials and NGOs mentioned that the uncertainty of the SEC rule's outcome due to it being challenged may make it harder for companies to move forward in implementing their due diligence process to address the SEC reporting requirements.

indicated that the SEC rule has also shaped and influenced initiatives to create a conflict-free supply chain by the International Conference of the Great Lakes Region (ICGLR) and the governments of the DRC and Rwanda. We provide a more detailed discussion later in this report on the ways in which companies required to report under the rule, in order to comply, are interacting with companies not required to report under the rule.

Stakeholder-Developed Initiatives May Increase Companies' Assurance That Conflict Minerals They Use Are Not Benefiting DRC Armed Groups

Stakeholder-Developed Initiatives May Aid Companies' Due Diligence Efforts

Some agency officials we interviewed stated that stakeholder-developed initiatives focused on sourcing of minerals may enhance companies' ability to achieve the SEC rule's desired outcome of denying armed groups in the DRC benefits from conflict minerals. As mentioned in our 2012 report, stakeholder-developed initiatives—which include the development of guidance documents, audit protocols, and in-region sourcing—support efforts by companies reporting to SEC under the rule to (1) conduct due diligence of their conflict minerals supply chain, (2) identify the source of conflict minerals within their supply chain, and (3) responsibly source conflict minerals. These initiatives can be classified as in-region or global, and some are now being expanded.

In-Region Sourcing Initiatives Focus on Tracing of Conflict Minerals

In-region sourcing initiatives, as we reported in 2012, may support responsible sourcing of conflict minerals from Central Africa and the identification of specific mines of origin for those minerals. Regional sourcing initiatives in the DRC and neighboring countries focus on tracing minerals from the mine to the mineral smelter or refiner by supporting a bagging and tagging program or some type of traceability scheme. Examples of such initiatives include the ITRI Tin Supply Chain Initiative (iTSCi) and the Conflict-Free Tin Initiative (CFTI). (See app. III for more detailed information on these and selected other in-region sourcing initiatives). The iTSCi initiative was developed by a tin industry association known as ITRI. The initiative supports responsible sourcing of tin, tantalum, and tungsten from Central Africa and was launched in

Rwanda in December 2010 and in the Katanga province of the DRC in March 2011. iTSCi expanded its activities in the Maniema province of the DRC in December 2012. We reported in 2012 that iTSCi is a traceability and due diligence program that creates auditable and verifiable chains of custody for tin, tantalum, and tungsten through (1) tagging and bagging of materials and the collection of tagging data and (2) regular incident reporting and continuous monitoring of mines and companies participating in the program. In October 2012, the Dutch government, with industry partners such as iTSCi, started the Conflict-Free Tin Initiative focused on conflict-free tin sourcing from South Kivu in the DRC, a region that is prone to insecurity and violence by illegal armed groups. This initiative is a traceability and due diligence mechanism that brings partners along the supply chain together, from mine to smelter to end-user. This also includes consumers as well as the DRC government and civil society[28] and uses the OECD due diligence guidance. According to an implementer, the progress of the initiative will depend on how the security situation in South Kivu develops.

While the in-region sourcing initiatives have focused on tin, tantalum, and tungsten to date, one of the most recent in-region initiatives in the DRC is through the Public-Private Alliance for Responsible Minerals Trade (PPA) and is focused on a pilot gold traceability scheme. In fall of 2012, Partnership Africa Canada began work on establishing an in-region gold traceability project partially funded by PPA. According to information from PPA, the project aims to create a traceable conflict-free mineral chain for artisanal gold from the eastern DRC, in the Orientale province, thus demonstrating the feasibility of creating artisanal gold chains with full traceability from mine site to gold refiner.

According to industry and agency officials, in-region sourcing programs can provide better economic incentive for miners to sell minerals that do not benefit armed groups. For example, iTSCi reported in February 2013 that the tin initiative in South Kivu had led to a number of immediate benefits for the local population, which depends on mining as its source of income. Specifically, the price paid to the miners for conflict-free minerals mined at the site had more than doubled. iTSCi further reported that the

---

[28]The World Bank defines the term "civil society" to refer to the wide array of nongovernmental and not-for-profit organizations that have a presence in public life, expressing the interests and values of their members or others, based on ethical, cultural, political, scientific, religious, or philanthropic considerations.

additional income had allowed the mining cooperatives to invest in basic equipment such as electricity generators and to improve productivity and working conditions. Additionally, some agency officials stated that in-region initiatives can help develop capacity in the DRC.

Global Sourcing Initiatives Affect Companies throughout the Supply Chain

We reported in 2012 that global sourcing initiatives may minimize the risk of minerals that have been exploited by illegal armed groups from entering the supply chain and support companies' efforts to identify the source of the conflict minerals across the supply chain around the world. (See app. III for more detailed information on selected global sourcing initiatives.) One such global initiative is the Conflict-Free Smelter Program, co-developed by the Global e-Sustainability Initiative (GeSI) and the Electronics Industry Citizenship Coalition (EICC). The Conflict-Free Smelter Program is a voluntary initiative in which an independent third party audits smelters' procurement activities——among other activities——and determines if the smelters demonstrated that the minerals they processed originated from conflict-free sources. Companies that can trace their conflict minerals supply chain back to compliant smelters or refiners can claim that the minerals in their products are from a smelter[29] whose processes reasonably assure conflict-free production.[30]

Industry experts we interviewed explained that if initiatives such as the Conflict-Free Smelter Program can result in smelters refining minerals that did not benefit armed groups, then companies can comply better with the SEC rule requirements and have more confidence in their supply chain sources. Specifically, one expert stated that companies that are conducting due diligence under the rule would not have to audit the smelter themselves, if the smelter has already been audited under the Conflict-Free Smelter Program. Agency officials, both in Washington, D.C., and in the DRC, reported that the Conflict Free Smelter Program seems to be a positive initiative since the more smelters are certified as conflict-free, the more beneficial this will be for companies reporting under the SEC rule.

---

[29]Smelters are the natural choke point in the supply chain—meaning that there are numerous sources of raw materials (ore) that flow into a smelter and numerous uses for the refined metals that leave the smelter.

[30]According to industry representatives, independent third-party audits for the Conflict-Free Smelter Program are lagging and thus cannot assure that minerals are conflict-free on future purchasing actions.

Overall, agency officials we interviewed stated that existing initiatives and traceability schemes on the ground in the DRC and neighboring countries have been yielding benefits of producing conflict-free minerals; however, according to these officials, more progress could be made in the responsible sourcing of conflict minerals from the region. Some industry experts also indicated that while progress has been made and the initiation or expansion of in-region sourcing initiatives is possible, factors such as the ones described below remain a concern.

Lack of Security, Inadequate Infrastructure, and Capacity Constraints in the DRC Could Affect Companies' Ability to Ensure Conflict-Free Sourcing of Minerals

Some agency officials as well as representatives we interviewed from NGOs, industry, and international organizations cited lack of security, inadequate infrastructure, and capacity constraints as factors that could affect the ability to expand on efforts to achieve conflict-free sourcing of minerals from the eastern DRC and thereby potentially contribute to armed groups benefiting from the conflict minerals trade. We also cited these same factors in our 2010 report and pointed out that these factors posed challenges to tracking the mines of origin for minerals artisanally mined in eastern DRC.[31] While officials we spoke to for this report discussed these factors in the context of the SEC rule, these factors are pre-existing regional challenges that pre-date both the Dodd Frank Act and the SEC conflict minerals rule.[32]

Lack of Security in Eastern DRC Could Hamper Sourcing Initiatives

Officials cited the lack of security, including weak governance, as a factor that could impact responsible sourcing from the DRC. The UN reported that the DRC government has been unable to exercise authority in eastern DRC, which has become more evident as illegal armed groups clashed in the Kivu provinces late in 2012. State also reported that lack of security has prevented the export of conflict-free minerals from certain areas in eastern DRC. Industry and NGO officials who work on the ground in the DRC pointed out that the threat from illegal armed groups poses a challenge to the conflict-free minerals initiatives operating in eastern DRC and the neighboring provinces. Although the mining sites are constantly monitored, the monitoring activities could be suspended at

---

[31]GAO-10-1030.

[32]The list of factors is not intended to be exhaustive and is based on views of experts and stakeholders. Additional factors may exist once the SEC rule has been in place for a longer period of time. We did not address how the challenges raised by the factors discussed can be mitigated or what progress the DRC government has made to address them because it was outside the scope of our review.

any time as the security situation evolves. For example, an NGO reported that tagging was suspended for days in July 2012 at an iTSCi site in the Katanga province because of the movement of armed groups in the vicinity of the mine sites; however, there were no reported cases of armed groups successfully taking control of the sites or directly exploiting minerals to fund activities.

In-region sourcing initiatives have operated in areas that have been vetted by various stakeholders and have the support of government and civil society actors. According to the UN Group of Experts on the Democratic Republic of the Congo (UNGoE), the security situation at tin, tantalum, and tungsten mining sites has improved and the trade of these minerals has become a much less important source of financing for armed groups. However, the UNGoE reported a "genuine risk that military actors would move their rackets to mining activities that were not closely supervised." They further reported that the gold trade is linked to armed groups and criminal networks in the Congolese armed forces. According to the UNGoE, lack of security at gold mining sites throughout eastern DRC remained widespread. Agency officials emphasized that armed groups still existed in the DRC despite the initiatives in place and would seek control of any significant revenue-producing activity in the region.

Some industry officials cited concerns about sourcing from the DRC, even through the in-region sourcing initiatives, because of the potential impact on brand reputation and financial risk. For example, a representative of a smelter indicated that if the company purchased minerals from a mine that is part of a traceability scheme that is deemed conflict-free but then illegal armed groups infiltrated and compromised the mine in the future, the company would not be able to say with certainty that the minerals it had purchased were conflict-free.

Limited Infrastructure Could Hamper Access to Mines

Officials cited limited infrastructure as a factor that could affect the creation or expansion of in-region sourcing initiatives. Officials from UNGoE and industry representatives we interviewed noted a lack of infrastructure in place that would enable companies to set up or expand operations in the DRC. Limited transportation and poor roads in eastern DRC also make it difficult to get to mine sites. For example, an agency official in the DRC commented that mines may be a day's walk from a main road. Also, an NGO reported that in selecting a potential pilot site for a traceability scheme, accessibility to the site by road was a key criterion and would involve using off-road vehicles due to the significant deterioration of roads leading to the mine. Moreover, according to an NGO representative, the remoteness of mines also makes it difficult for

DRC mine officials to validate mines and ensure that the mines have not been compromised by armed groups. Furthermore, State officials indicated that the lack of infrastructure prevents trade initiatives from developing economies of scale and expanding.

Lack of Capacity Could Impact Due Diligence

Officials we interviewed cited the lack of technical, economic, and political capacity as another factor that may affect the creation or expansion of in-region sourcing initiatives focused on responsible sourcing in the DRC and neighboring countries. In 2013, the OECD reported that while the understanding of responsible sourcing is "high for those actors in the DRC and Rwanda who have participated in such initiatives, the same is not true for state agents" in the country.[33] The OECD report also pointed out that Ugandan and Burundian government officials and other entities lack technical understanding of due diligence requirements. Some NGO officials stated that lack of capacity can impact the due diligence process in the supply chain, especially if the numbers of trained mining agents is insufficient. For example, some agency officials and an NGO reported that the DRC does not have enough mine agents to certify the mines, of which there may be over 2,000 in eastern DRC alone, or even to negotiate and manage mining contracts. Moreover, an NGO official stated that mines need to be reinspected every 6 to 12 months in order to ensure proper due diligence in accordance with OECD and ICGLR guidance; however, the NGO official stated that the DRC government does not have the capacity to inspect at such frequency.

Some agency officials and officials we interviewed from industry, NGOs, and international organizations also commented that the DRC government lacks capacity to mitigate corruption and smuggling. The lack of capacity can impact due diligence and can contribute to illegal minerals trade and cross-border smuggling. For example, the UN reported that illegal trade of minerals undermines the exercise of due diligence in the DRC and affects the credibility of due diligence-based certification and traceability systems.[34] According to some industry experts, mining agents

---

[33]Organisation for Economic Co-operation and Development, *Upstream Implementation of the OECD Due Diligence Guidance for Responsible Supply Chains of Minerals from Conflict-Affected and High-Risk Areas: Final Report on One-Year Pilot Implementation of the Supplement on Tin, Tantalum, and Tungsten* (OECD: January 2013).

[34]Letter dated 12 November 2012 from the Chair of the Security Council to resolution 1533 (2004) concerning the Democratic Republic of the Congo addressed to the President of the Security Council (S/2012/843), the United Nations Security Council (Nov. 15, 2012).

may not be properly compensated, due to the lack of governance in eastern DRC, and may look for other ways to earn money, which could involve colluding with illegal armed groups.

With regard to smuggling, the OECD reported that as long as there are no traceability or certification schemes in place that cover the whole region, and most notably, the Kivu provinces, Uganda, and Burundi, smuggling and contamination of clean materials will continue to pose a threat to formalization of the artisanal mining sector and due diligence initiatives. According to a 2012 UNGoE report, several tons of gold worth hundreds of millions of dollars are smuggled from the eastern DRC through neighboring countries, where it is ultimately smelted and sold to jewelers in markets, such as the United Arab Emirates. Representatives from some industry associations that we interviewed stated that armed groups and criminal elements have shifted efforts to gold mines because it is relatively easy to smuggle gold because of its size. Furthermore, gold's high value in the market makes it more viable for smuggling than tin, tantalum, and tungsten.

Many Companies Not Required to Report to SEC under the Conflict Minerals Rule Will Likely Be Affected; Limited Aggregated Information about Them Exists

Even companies that are not required to file disclosures under SEC's conflict minerals rule will likely be affected by the rule. These companies may supply components or parts that contain conflict minerals to companies reporting to SEC under the rule and may be asked by such companies to provide information specifying the origin of the minerals. Aside from the supply chain relationship, while information is publicly available about some smelters and refiners, there is little aggregated information available about companies that do not report to SEC under the rule but may trade in conflict minerals.

Companies Not Required to Report to SEC under the Rule May Provide Information on the Origin of Conflict Minerals in Their Products to Companies That Will Report to SEC under the Rule

Companies Not Required to Report to SEC under the Rule May Supply Products That May Contain Conflict Minerals to SEC-Reporting Companies under the Rule

Companies that are not required to report to SEC under the rule may supply products that contain conflict minerals to SEC-reporting companies under the rule. SEC relied on estimates provided by a commentator indicating that 278,000 suppliers—most of which would be companies that would not report to SEC under the rule—could be indirectly impacted by the rule. Moreover, the release contains an estimate that each of the nearly 6,000 companies that could be directly impacted by the rule has roughly 1,000 first-tier suppliers, on average.[35] These suppliers, including first-tier suppliers, could provide products that contain conflict minerals to companies required to report to SEC under the rule. Examples of these products include tin solder for joining metal, tantalum capacitors for storing energy in cellular phones, tungsten carbide for hardened cutting tools, or gold plating for wires to increase durability and resistance to corrosion. The first-tier supplier has a direct commercial relationship with the original equipment manufacturer, meaning the first-tier supplier sells materials or component parts, which have been aggregated by suppliers throughout the supply chain, to the original equipment manufacturer for final assembly. According to an industry official, in general, component parts manufacturers construct

---

[35]The actual number of first-tier suppliers is unknown, and organizations that commented on the release provided varying estimates on the number of first-tier suppliers that could potentially be affected by the SEC rule. As cited in the SEC release, commentators provided estimates indicating that SEC-reporting companies under the rule averaged nearly 160 to 10,000 first-tier suppliers, each. In addition, another commentator estimated that SEC-reporting companies averaged 1,060 first-tier suppliers each. After accounting for redundancies, because a supplier may be in more than one supply chain, SEC revised the number of potentially affected suppliers, provided by one commentator, to 278,000 suppliers.

individual parts—such as capacitors, engine parts, circuit boards, and other components—and assemble them into more complex components.

Using an electronics company as a model, processed metals move through several suppliers that manufacture component parts after the smelter—first to circuit board and computer chip manufacturers, then to cellular phone and other electronics manufacturers, and finally to the brand-name electronics company, which is the original equipment manufacturer that manufactures products recognizable to the consumer, such as cellular phones, tablets, and laptop computers. Beyond the first-tier supplier, there are tier 2-, 3-, 4-, or higher-tiered suppliers that, beginning with the raw materials from the smelter or refiner, manufacture component parts that are assembled into more complex component parts as they move from higher- to lower-tiered suppliers in the supply chain, to the first-tier supplier, and finally to the original equipment manufacturer.[37] See figure 4 for a simplified version of the supply chain, and the tiered structure of suppliers.

---

[36]For the purpose of the estimate, SEC estimated that the rule would affect 5,551 of 13,545 domestic issuers that file form 10-K, 377 of 942 foreign private issuers that file form 20-F, and 66 of 205 Canadian issuers that file form 40-F, annually. According to the adopting release for the rule, SEC based its estimate of 5,994 affected companies on the number of issuers that fall under all Standard Industrial Classification (SIC) codes that SEC staff believed were most likely to manufacture or contract to manufacture products with necessary conflict minerals.

[37]SEC estimates that a number of SEC-reporting companies under the rule may be original equipment manufacturers and first-tier suppliers, although SEC-reporting companies under the rule could exist anywhere on the supply chain.

Figure 4: Simplified Conflict Minerals Supply Chain Showing Supplier Tiers

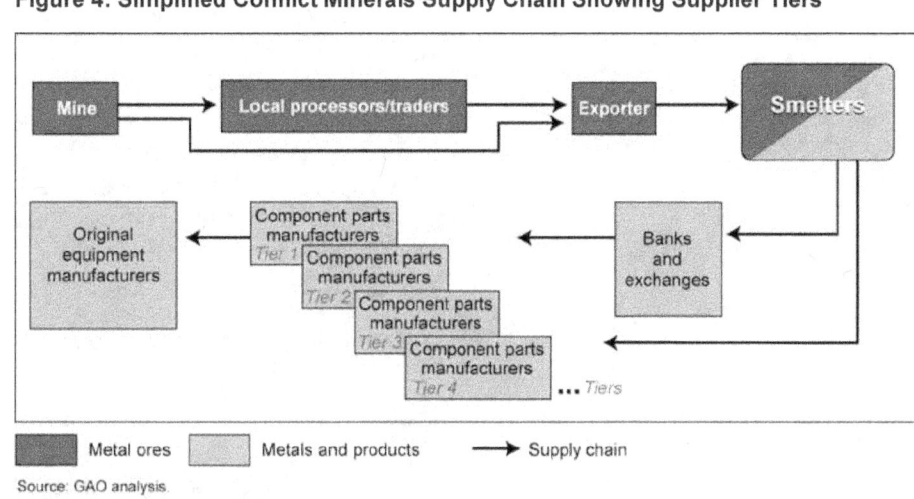

Source: GAO analysis

While many companies will likely be directly or indirectly impacted by the rule, some companies that use conflict minerals may not be, partly because (1) the companies are not issuers that are required to file with SEC under the Securities Exchange Act, and (2) these same companies potentially do not sell components or parts to a company that will be required to report to SEC under the rule. Industry and consulting firm representatives have differing views on the number of companies that purchase conflict minerals from the DRC and adjoining countries but may not be impacted by the rule.

SEC-Reporting Companies under the Rule May Request Information on the Origin of Conflict Minerals in Products They Receive from Their Suppliers

Suppliers that provide products that may contain conflict minerals to companies required to report to SEC under the rule may provide information on the minerals' origins to those reporting companies that request it. The SEC release does not specify the steps and outcomes for the reasonable country of origin inquiry, and indicates that such a determination depends on each issuer's facts and circumstances. However, in conducting a country of origin inquiry, issuers may inquire of their suppliers the origin of any conflict minerals in the products. According to the release, the issuer's inquiry must be reasonably designed to determine whether any of its conflict minerals originated in the DRC and adjoining countries, and must be performed in good faith. If, after this inquiry, the issuer has a reason to believe that its conflict minerals may have originated in the DRC and adjoining countries, the issuer proceeds to exercising due diligence. Industry associations such as the EICC and GeSI have created templates for companies to use when contacting suppliers to inquire about the types and origins of conflict minerals in a given product.[38] For example, companies required to report under the rule could submit the inquiries to their first-tier suppliers. Those suppliers could either provide the reporting company with sufficient information or initiate the inquiry process up the supply chain, such as by distributing the inquiries to suppliers at the next tier—tier 2 suppliers. The tier 2 suppliers could inquire up the supply chain to additional suppliers, until the inquiries arrive at the smelter. Smelters then could provide the suppliers with information about the origin of the conflict minerals. Figure 5 illustrates the flow of information up the supply chain.

Figure 5: Flow of Supply Chain Inquiries from the Original Equipment Manufacturers to the Mine

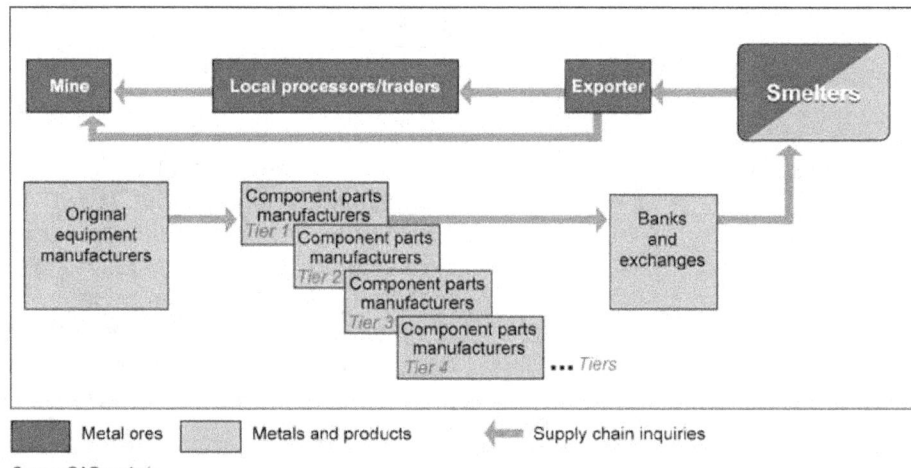

Source: GAO analysis.

As discussed earlier, smelters have various means to preclude untraced minerals from entering their supply, such as participation in the iTSCi initiative and the Conflict Free Smelters Program. According to smelting industry representatives, these initiatives and certifications have reduced the burden of responding to the multiple amounts of inquiries many smelters have already received from suppliers.

---

[38]According to EICC and GeSI, as of April 30, 2013, the EICC and GeSI activities are now under the Conflict Free Sourcing Initiative, which is an expanded initiative of the EICC and GeSI Extractives Work Group that includes more stakeholders and a wider range of industry sectors supporting the sourcing of conflict-free minerals.

Officials from consulting firms and industry associations that we spoke with told us that many companies that will respond under the rule have started contacting their first-tier suppliers and providing them with country of origin inquiries. According to these officials, several of these companies that have submitted inquiries to their suppliers have experienced challenges, which include identifying suppliers beyond the first-tier suppliers, because for original equipment manufacturers, suppliers beyond the first tier are less visible. As discussed earlier, original equipment manufacturers purchase component parts primarily from their first-tier suppliers and do not have direct commercial relationships with suppliers in higher tiers of the supply chain. According to industry representatives and agency officials, these challenges may impact how companies file under the rule. For example, as previously discussed, the SEC rule allows companies to disclose their products as "DRC conflict undeterminable." This provision allows companies to state that the source of the conflict minerals in their products, and the likelihood that the conflict minerals benefited or financed armed groups from the DRC and adjoining countries, could not be determined after having conducted due diligence to obtain that information from their suppliers. For the reporting period beginning January 1, 2013, companies may use this provision for 4 years for smaller reporting companies or 2 years for all other reporting companies. Although the number of companies required to report under the rule that may utilize the "DRC conflict undeterminable" provision is unknown, SEC officials and representatives of industry associations and consulting firms anticipate that many companies required to report under the rule will utilize the provision based on the results of their due diligence efforts.

Representatives from industry and consulting firms that we interviewed stated that the purchasing power of issuing companies under the rule may influence their suppliers to provide information on the source of any conflict minerals in their products when requested. According to an industry representative, since companies that report to SEC under the rule tend to be large, mature corporations with great purchasing power in their respective industries, it would be difficult for suppliers to ignore their request for information on the origin of conflict minerals in products the suppliers provide to them. For example, jewelry industry representatives told us that they have advised their members, which are primarily small, independent jewelry companies not required to report to SEC under the rule, to respond to any requests from customers seeking information on the origin of conflict minerals in products they supply, because the risk of not responding could result in a loss of business for those companies.

Information Is Publicly
Available about Smelters and
Refiners, and the Types of
Conflict Minerals They Use

Some information is publicly available about smelters and refiners, and their involvement in the conflict minerals supply chain. According to SEC officials, while smelters and refiners are not exempted from the SEC rule, most of these suppliers will likely not be required to report to SEC under the rule because of their filing status.[39] Smelter and refiners are considered the choke-point of the conflict minerals supply chain, as previously discussed, and comprise a small portion of the overall number of suppliers in the conflict minerals supply chain that may be impacted by the SEC rule. While it is not possible to determine the universe of suppliers that would not be required to report under the rule, smelters and refiners are a more identifiable population for which there is some aggregated information, such as the types of conflict minerals they use, and their location.[40] We found the following information on smelters and refiners:

- *Smelters and refiners constitute a small but important portion of suppliers that likely will not file a conflict minerals report under the SEC rule.* Organizations have estimated the number of smelters and refiners around the world to be nearly 500; however, the actual number of smelters and refiners of conflict minerals is unknown. We aggregated publicly available information on smelters and refiners from lists compiled by the EICC and GeSI, the OECD, and the London Bullion Market Association (LBMA), which provided information on 278 smelters and refiners. As we have previously discussed, roughly 278,000 suppliers could be affected by the rule, based on the estimate provided to SEC. Of the 278 smelters of tin, tantalum, tungsten, and refiners of gold that we were able to identify, the majority (271) of these companies would likely not be required to report under the rule.
- *Over half of the smelters and refiners of the conflict minerals we identified were located in three countries.* Of the 278 smelters and refiners of tin, tantalum, tungsten, and gold that we were able to identify, more than half (156) were located in three countries: China (82), Japan (39), and Indonesia (35). According to industry

[39]According to SEC officials, since most of these companies do not file reports with SEC under Section 13(a) or 15(d) of the Securities Exchange Act, they would not be required to report under the rule.

[40]We are reporting information we found and analyzed on smelters and refiners to address the mandated question concerning available information about entities that use conflict minerals and do not report to SEC under the rule.

representatives, participation in due diligence efforts of smelters and refiners from these countries, particularly China and Indonesia, is critical in assisting companies with fulfilling the reporting requirements of the SEC rule. Several organizations, including an NGO, and representatives from government and industry, are conducting outreach to smelters to provide information on the SEC rule in an effort to increase participation from smelters and refiners from these countries. For more information on the location of smelters and refiners we identified in our analysis, see figure 6.

Figure 6: Number of Smelters and Refiners of Conflict Minerals We Identified, by Country

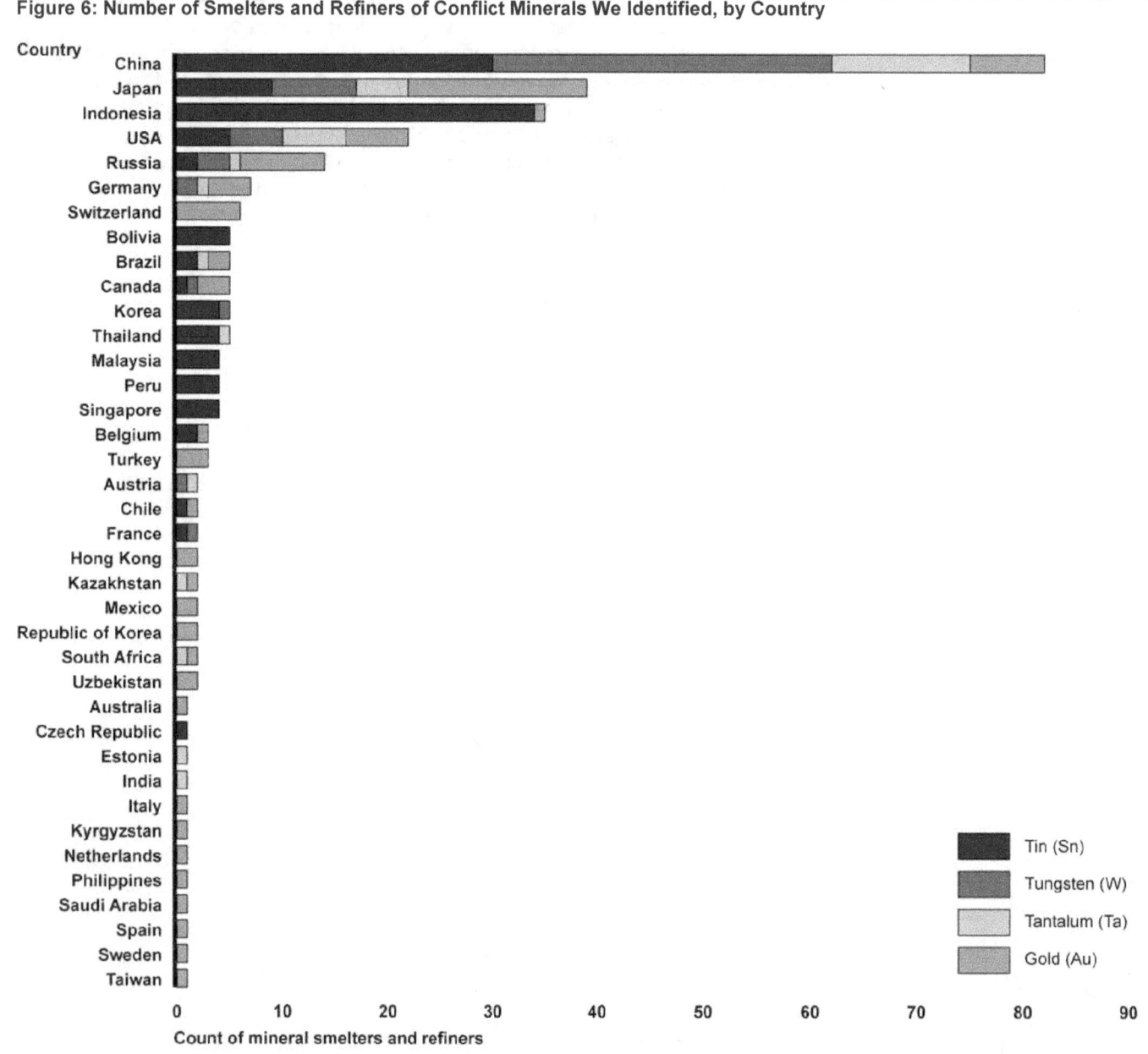

Source: GAO analysis of smelter information provided by the EICC-GeSI, OECD, and the LBMA.

Note: Eight smelters and refiners in our analysis processed more than one conflict mineral, resulting in duplicative counting in 21 cases. In addition, some smelters and refiners have operations in several countries.

GAO-13-689 SEC Conflict Minerals Rule

- *Many smelters and refiners of conflict minerals in our analysis processed tin.* Of the 278 smelters and refiners in our analysis, we were able to identify 113 that processed tin, followed by gold (78), tungsten (54), and tantalum (33). Furthermore, over half (64 of 113) of the tin smelters in our analysis were located in China (30) or Indonesia (34). In addition, over 67 percent of global production comes from mines in China and Indonesia, according to U.S. Geological Survey data. Tin and its derivatives have wide applications and are used in manufacturing a variety of products, including tin soldering for joining pipes, coatings for steel containers, and a wide range of tin chemical applications, according to the U.S. Geological Survey. According to industry and consulting firm representatives, around 12 to 15 smelters process nearly 80 percent of the world's tin.
- *Most smelters and refiners in our analysis did not have a conflict minerals policy publicly available.* Of the 278 smelters and refiners we were able to identify, 63 had a conflict minerals policy publicly available on their website. Of the 63 smelters with a conflict minerals policy publicly available, 26 smelters had successfully completed a Conflict Free Smelter Program audit and were designated as "conflict-free" by the EICC and GeSI,[41] while several had reportedly followed some sort of due diligence, such as the OECD Due Diligence Guidance or the LMBA Responsible Gold Guidance.[42] Other smelters in our analysis had posted policies on their website stating that the company only sources conflict minerals outside of the conflict areas of the DRC and adjoining countries. We were unable to identify a website for 86 of the 278 smelters in our analysis, and 129 of the 278

---

[41]Five additional tin smelters have successfully completed a Conflict Free Smelter Program audit, bringing the number of certified "conflict-free" smelters to 35; however, the EICC and GeSI has yet to identify these smelters publicly, including the location of the smelters, due to binding non-disclosure agreements with the smelters.

[42]LMBA created the Responsible Gold Guidance for Good Delivery Refiners to combat systematic or widespread abuses of human rights, and to avoid contributing to conflict, among other abuses, according to the guidance. In addition, the guidance follows the five steps framework for risk-based due diligence of the OECD Due Diligence Guidance for Responsible Supply Chains of Minerals from Conflict-Affected and High-Risk Areas adopted on December 15, 2010 and follows the requirements detailed in the OECD Gold Supplement adopted on July 17, 2012. Since January 2012, the LBMA has required all Good Delivery Gold Refiners to comply with the Responsible Gold Guidance.

smelters had no conflict minerals policy publicly available on their website.[43]

Some information is publicly available on companies that use conflict minerals but are not required to report under the rule, as in the case of many smelters and refiners we were able to identify. However, data for the universe of these companies are limited. Specifically, based on our analysis, aggregated data on the types of conflict minerals in the products manufactured by these companies as well as information on how such companies source their conflict minerals are not available, except for a few companies. For example, several of these companies provide information publicly about their continued participation in initiatives that source conflict minerals from the DRC, and have agreed to purchase conflict minerals, such as tin and tantalum, from closely monitored sources through initiatives such as iTSCi and the Solutions for Hope, as previously mentioned.[44] However, according to agency and international organization officials, in some instances buyers from small firms, mainly from East Asia, are on the ground in the DRC and adjoining countries, and continue to purchase untraced minerals as well as minerals that have been smuggled out of the DRC into adjoining countries. In addition, according to an industry representative, it may be difficult to identify information on these companies because they tend to be small and serve very specific markets.

---

[43]We were unable to identify a website for 86 of the 278 smelters in our analysis, and therefore were unable to determine whether these companies have policies regarding procuring conflict minerals from the DRC and adjoining countries. The inability to locate some websites of smelters in our analysis could be linked to factors such as language as well as company names and websites that may contain characters not found in the Roman alphabet. According to an official with the EICC and GeSI, some smelters may have such small operations at the mine site in remote locations that they do not create websites.

[44]Solutions for Hope is a "closed-pipeline" initiative to trace the flow of tantalum from the mine to the end-use company.

GAO-13-689 SEC Conflict Minerals Rule

Little Additional Information on the Rate of Sexual Violence in Eastern DRC and Neighboring Countries Has Become Available since GAO's 2012 Report

Since our 2012 report, one population-based survey providing data on the rate of sexual violence has been published in Uganda, and one is under way in the DRC; during the same period, no similar surveys have been conducted in Rwanda or Burundi. We also found some additional case file data available on sexual violence for all four countries. However, as we reported in 2011, case file data on sexual violence are not suitable for estimating a rate of sexual violence.

Since GAO's 2012 Report, One Population-Based Survey on the Rate of Sexual Violence Has Been Published in Uganda and One Is Planned for DRC

We found that one new population-based survey on the rate of sexual violence has been conducted since our 2012 report[45]—the 2011 Uganda Demographic and Health Survey (DHS), published in August 2012. According to the survey, "28 percent of women and 9 percent of men age 15-49 report that they have experienced sexual violence at least once in their lifetime." These national estimates are based on a random sample. Since we first reported on sexual violence in our 2011 report, we have identified six other population-based surveys that provided data on the rate of sexual violence in these countries.

[45]GAO-12-763.

In reviewing whether there had been updates to any of the previous surveys conducted, we found that the authors of the McGill study, a population-based survey conducted in eastern DRC that was highlighted in our 2011 report, had no plans to conduct a follow-up survey. We found that fieldwork for a DHS for the DRC is expected to launch in August 2013, with data expected around September 2014.

Figure 7: Population-Based Surveys That Estimate the Rate of Sexual Violence in Eastern DRC, Rwanda, and Uganda

By publication date

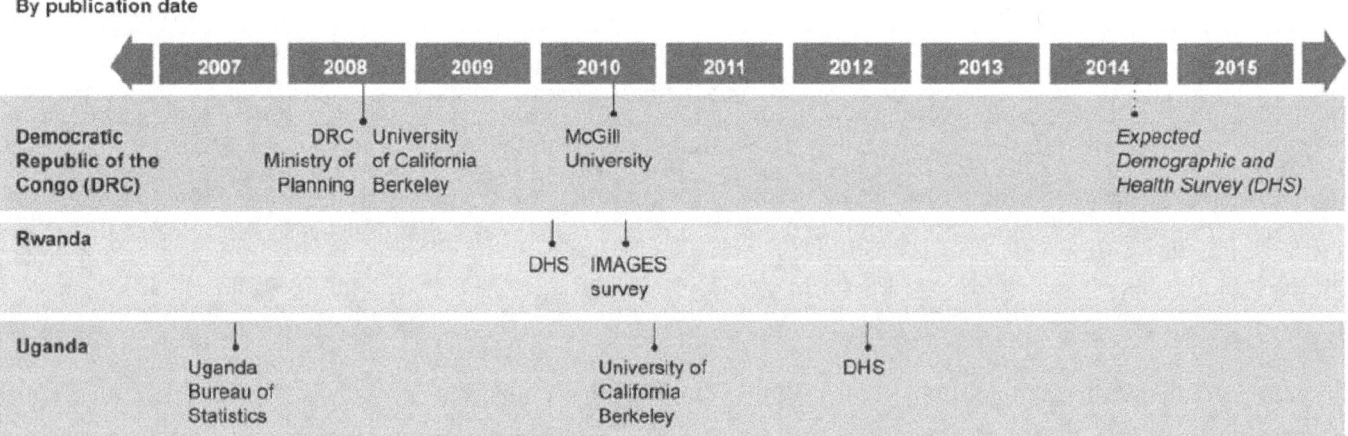

Source: GAO analysis.

Notes: For our analysis of the quality of the surveys, refer to our 2011 report (GAO-11-702). For DHS surveys covered after our 2011 report, we found that these surveys are weighted, present confidence intervals, and adhere to other survey standards. During our search for studies published since our 2012 report, we discovered the IMAGES survey, which we had not previously reported on in either our 2011 or 2012 report.

We also found a team of two organizations that released estimates in 2010 based on survey data of sexual violence in Rwanda. Sonke Gender Justice Network and Promundo-US conducted a probability cluster sample in 2010 as part of its IMAGES survey and found that "57 percent of women reported having experienced gender-based violence committed by a partner" and "17 percent of men experienced sexual violence when they were a child." However, this survey was not weighted to reflect unequal probabilities of selection, and it does not contain confidence intervals. Therefore, we are not able to assess the accuracy or precision of the estimates.

Some Additional Case File Data Has Become Available on Sexual Violence since GAO's 2012 Report

Following up on our 2011 and 2012 reports, we asked U.S. and UN agencies as well as researchers and NGOs if they had any updated case file data. In April 2013, State submitted its annual country reports on human rights practices to Congress, which provided case file information pertaining to sexual violence in the DRC and neighboring countries. The 2012 *Department of State Human Rights Reports* reported the following:

- In DRC, the Ministry of Gender reported 10,037 cases of sexual- and gender-based violence in 2011 in eastern DRC.
- In Rwanda, prosecutors reported that they investigated 351 cases of rape in 2012. Of those 351 cases, 109 were filed in courts, 143 were dropped, and 99 were pending investigation.
- In Uganda, 520 cases of rape were reported in 2011, of which 269 were tried.
- In Burundi, Centre Seruka, a clinic for rape victims averaged 121 rape cases per month between January and September 2012.

Various UN entities reported other case file data. In March 2013, the UN Secretary-General reported that 764 people had become victims of sexual violence in eastern DRC from December 2011 and through November 2012.[46] In May 2013, the UN Joint Human Rights Office reported that an armed group committed 135 cases of sexual violence from November 20, 2012 through November 30, 2012. Furthermore, in December 2012, the UN Office for the Coordination of Humanitarian Affairs reported 70 rapes in Minova, a town in eastern DRC, from November 30 through December 4, 2012. Because case file data are not

---

[46]United Nations Security Council, *Sexual Violence in Conflict: Report of the Secretary-General*, A/67/792-S/2013/149 (New York, NY: Mar 14, 2013).

aggregated across various sources and the extent to which various reports overlap is unclear, it is difficult to obtain complete data on case files or even a sense of magnitude. One shortcoming of both case file data and surveys is that time frames, locales, and definitions of sexual violence are not consistent across data collection operations. As we reported in 2011, case file data on sexual violence are not suitable for estimating a rate of sexual violence because case file data are not based on a random sample and the results of analyzing these data are not generalizable.

Agency Comments and Our Evaluation

We provided a draft of this report to SEC, State, and USAID, for their review and comment. SEC, State, and USAID provided technical comments, which we incorporated in this report as appropriate. We also provided relevant portions of the draft of this report to relevant external stakeholders for their technical comment. We received technical comments from some of these stakeholders, which we incorporated throughout this report as appropriate.

We are sending copies of this report to appropriate congressional committees. The report is also available at no charge on the GAO website at http://www.gao.gov/.

If you or your staffs have any questions about this report, please contact me at (202) 512-4802 or evansl@gao.gov. Contact points for our Offices of Congressional Relations and Public Affairs may be found on the last page of this report. GAO staff who made major contributions to this report are listed in appendix IV.

Lawrance L. Evans, Jr.
Director, International Affairs and Trade

List of Addressees

The Honorable Barbara Mikulski
Chairwoman
The Honorable Richard Shelby
Ranking Member
Committee on Appropriations
United States Senate

The Honorable Tim Johnson
Chairman
The Honorable Mike Crapo
Ranking Member
Committee on Banking, Housing, and Urban Affairs
United States Senate

The Honorable Max Baucus
Chairman
The Honorable Orrin G. Hatch
Ranking Member
Committee on Finance
United States Senate

The Honorable Robert Menendez
Chairman
The Honorable Bob Corker
Ranking Member
Committee on Foreign Relations
United States Senate

The Honorable Hal Rogers
Chairman
The Honorable Nita Lowey
Ranking Member
Committee on Appropriations
House of Representatives

The Honorable Jeb Hensarling
Chairman
The Honorable Maxine Waters
Ranking Member
Committee on Financial Services
House of Representatives

The Honorable Ed Royce
Chairman
The Honorable Eliot Engel
Ranking Member
Committee on Foreign Affairs
House of Representatives

The Honorable Dave Camp
Chairman
The Honorable Sander Levin
Ranking Member
Committee on Ways and Means
House of Representatives

Appendix I: Objectives, Scope, and Methodology

To describe factors that may impact whether the Securities and Exchange Commission's (SEC) conflict minerals rule denies armed groups in the Democratic Republic of the Congo (DRC) and adjoining countries benefits from conflict minerals, we interviewed officials from SEC, the Department of State (State), and the United States Agency for International Development (USAID), as well as representatives from international organizations, nongovernmental organizations (NGO), industry associations, consulting firms, and smelters and refiners of tin, tantalum, tungsten, and gold to get their views on the final SEC rule as well as any impacting factors. We chose the experts and stakeholders we interviewed to capture a range of perspectives about the types of minerals traded and because we had established contacts with these entities on our last review. In addition, some of the stakeholders we talked to have been working on the ground in the DRC. These experts and stakeholders constitute a nongeneralizable sample. The information gathered cannot be generalized and cannot be used to infer views of other experts or stakeholders cognizant of conflict minerals issues. We reviewed Section 1502 of the Dodd-Frank Wall Street Reform and Consumer Protection Act (Pub. L. No. 111-203); reports and other documents from relevant U.S. agencies, such as SEC's final conflict minerals rule, press releases, and statements; reports issued by the UN Group of Experts on the Democratic Republic of the Congo (UNGoE) and the Organisation for Economic Co-operation and Development (OECD); as well as documents and reports from industry associations and NGOs. We did not travel to the DRC or speak with government officials in the DRC but obtained perspectives on issues from some stakeholders who operate in the DRC.

To identify and describe available information about entities that use conflict minerals and do not report to SEC under the rule, we interviewed officials from SEC, State, and USAID, as well as representatives from international organizations, NGOs, industry associations, consulting firms, and smelters and refiners of tin, tantalum, tungsten, and gold to get their views on the extent to which information is publicly available on companies that are not required to report under the rule that may use conflict minerals in their products, and the source of the conflict minerals. We reviewed and analyzed reports and other documents from organizations such as the OECD, London Bullion Market Association (LBMA), and the Electronics Industry Citizenship Coalition and the Global e-Sustainability Initiative (EICC and GeSI), as well as documents and reports from industry associations and NGOs. In addition, we conducted searches in the Nexis database using selected Standard Industrial Classification (SIC) codes listed under the Manufacturing division. Overall, there were 20 subcategories under the Manufacturing division of

SIC codes, which include subcategories such as Tobacco Products;
Paper and Allied Products; and Electronic and Other Electrical Equipment
and Components, Except Computer Equipment. We selected SIC codes
under the Manufacturing division for industries that have a higher
likelihood of using conflict minerals in their product, such as Electronic
and Other Electrical Equipment and Components, Except Computer
Equipment. Through the database analysis, we were able to determine
the filing status, location, revenue, and industry classification of the
companies. We were unable to determine the types of products the
companies produced, and the types of conflict minerals potentially used in
the manufacturing process of their products. Because SIC codes do not
indicate specific products, we were unable to use the Nexis data to
develop an aggregate description of entities that use conflict minerals but
do not report to SEC under the rule.

We compiled a list of smelters and refiners—which are a smaller universe
of companies that are primarily not required to report under the rule—
from the EICC and GeSI's Conflict Minerals Reporting Template and
Dashboard, OECD's *Final Downstream Report On One-Year Pilot
Implementation of the Supplement on Tin, Tantalum, and Tungsten*, and
the LBMA's Good Delivery List. The data were current as of March 15,
2013. We selected these smelters and refiners because information is
publicly available on the types of minerals these smelters and refiners
process; however, we did not conduct an audit to verify how these entities
sourced materials for processing. To compile our list of smelters and
refiners, we reviewed and compared the lists from each source to identify
and delete duplicate smelters and refiners. Additional duplicates were
identified and deleted as a result of Internet searches using the names of
the smelters and refiners. While we made efforts to eliminate duplicate
information where possible, smelters and refiners may be listed under
different names, and therefore, some duplicate information may exist in
the data. Information included in the list of smelters from the EICC and
GeSI, OECD, and LMBA included (1) the location of the smelter or
refiner, (2) the types of minerals smelted or refined, and (3) the due
diligence guidance reportedly followed, in some cases. We identified 278
smelters and refiners of tin, tantalum, tungsten, and gold, and analyzed
any publicly available information—mainly information posted on the
companies' websites or information provided on the websites of
organizations such as the EICC and GeSI or the LBMA—on their
practices and policies for sourcing conflict minerals. This analysis
included examining websites of 192 of 278 smelters and refiners to
identify the types of due diligence guidance they reported to use to
determine the country of origin of their conflict minerals sources. We were

unable to identify the websites for 86 smelters or refiners on our list, which could have been the result of a smelter not possessing a website, or differing translations of company names from foreign characters—such as Chinese script or the Cyrillic alphabet—to the Roman alphabet. Additional limitations included our sample of 278 smelters and refiners, as organizations have estimated that the number of smelters and refiners is nearly 500, particularly if smaller smelters and refiners that process ores into metals at the mine site are included. These smelters and refiners, or secondary smelters, often have small operations and may not have a website, according to an industry representative. Furthermore, the number of gold refiners could potentially be much larger, considering that little equipment and space is required to refine gold, depending on the quality; and gold can be refined at the mine site. The 278 smelters and refiners we were able to identify may not be representative of others, and the information we report about these 278 cannot be generalized to other smelters and refiners of tin, tantalum, tungsten, and gold.

In response to a mandate in the Dodd-Frank Wall Street Reform and Consumer Protection Act that GAO submit an annual report that assesses the rate of sexual violence in war-torn areas of the DRC and adjoining countries, we identified and assessed any additional published information available on sexual violence in war-torn eastern DRC, as well as three neighboring countries that border eastern DRC—Rwanda, Uganda, and Burundi—since our 2012 report on sexual violence in these areas.[1] During the course of our review, we interviewed officials from State and USAID and interviewed NGO representatives and researchers to discuss the collection of sexual violence-related data—including population-based surveys and case file data—in the DRC and adjoining countries. Specifically, we followed up with researchers and representatives from those groups we interviewed for our prior review on sexual violence rates in eastern DRC and neighboring countries, including officials from the United Nations Population Fund, United Nations High Commissioner for Refugees, United Nations Special Representative to the Secretary-General on Sexual Violence in Conflict; and representatives from the Harvard Humanitarian Initiative and others. We also conducted Internet literature searches to identify new academic articles containing any additional data on sexual violence.

---

[1]GAO, *Conflict Minerals Disclosure Rule: SEC's Actions and Stakeholder-Developed Initiatives*, GAO-12-763 (Washington, D.C.: July 16, 2012). We did not include information on studies or reports that were preliminary.

We conducted this performance audit from November 2012 to July 2013 in accordance with generally accepted government auditing standards. Those standards require that we plan and perform the audit to obtain sufficient, appropriate evidence to provide a reasonable basis for our findings and conclusions based on our audit objectives. We believe that the evidence obtained provides a reasonable basis for our findings and conclusions based on our audit objectives.

Appendix II: SEC's Flowchart Summary of the Disclosure Process for the Final Conflict Minerals Rule

The Securities and Exchange Commission (SEC) issued a flowchart summary of the final rule to guide SEC-reporting companies affected by the rule through the disclosure process (see figure 8). In general, the process shows that an SEC-reporting company needs to (1) determine whether its manufactured products contain conflict minerals; (2) determine whether conflict minerals are necessary to the product and, if so, whether the conflict minerals originated in the DRC or an adjoining country; and (3) possibly conduct due diligence and potentially provide a Conflict Minerals Report.

Appendix II: SEC's Flowchart Summary of the
Disclosure Process for the Final Conflict
Minerals Rule

Figure 8: SEC's Flowchart Summary of the Final Conflict Minerals Rule

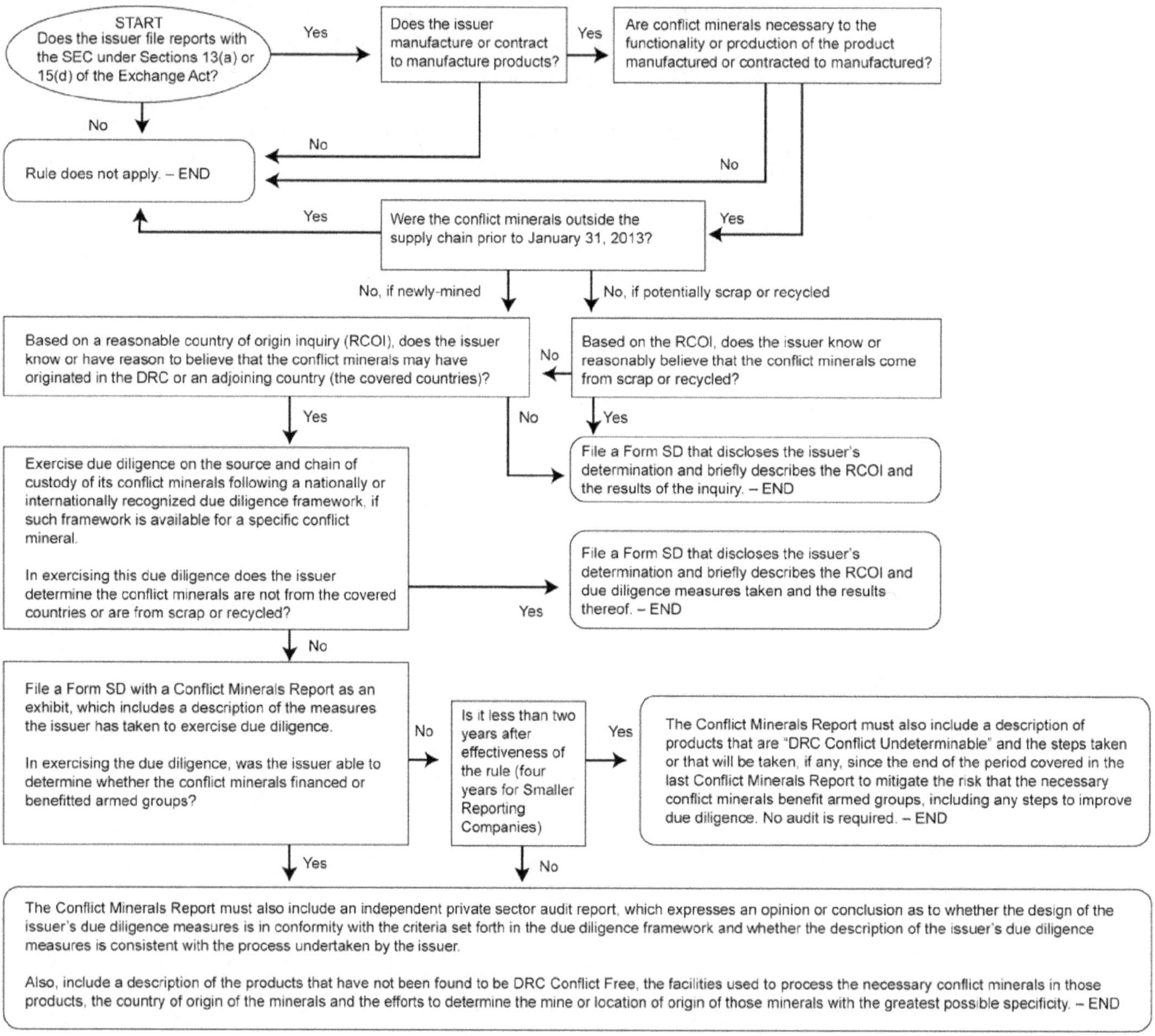

Source: SEC.

Note: SEC indicated that the flowchart is intended to be used as a guide and that issuers should refer to the text in the rule for a more comprehensive description of the rule's requirements.

Appendix III: Updates of Global and In-Region Sourcing Initiatives

In our 2012 report, we discussed a number of initiatives that various stakeholders developed and implemented that may help companies reporting to the Securities and Exchange Commission (SEC) and their suppliers comply with SEC's conflict minerals disclosure rule. For this report, we updated information pertaining to some of these global and in-region sourcing initiatives.[1]

Global Sourcing Initiatives

OECD Due Diligence Guidance

The Organisation for Economic Co-operation and Development (OECD) adopted the OECD Due Diligence Guidance for Responsible Supply Chains of Minerals from Conflict-Affected and High-Risk Areas (hereafter referred to as OECD Due Diligence Guidance) to promote accountability and transparency in conflict minerals supply chains.[2] The OECD Due Diligence Guidance and the corresponding supplements provide detailed guidance for companies operating in and sourcing minerals from conflict areas. In addition to the basic framework, OECD developed two supplements—one on tin, tantalum, and tungsten and the other on gold—to provide companies with specific guidance relevant to the conflict minerals supply chains. To increase awareness of and to develop emerging practices for implementing the OECD Due Diligence Guidance and the supplement on tin, tantalum, and tungsten, OECD conducted implementation pilot projects. In January 2013, OECD issued the final downstream report, which focuses on how companies implement due diligence in the supply chains of tin, tantalum, and tungsten, and the final upstream report, which provides an overall assessment of the progress

---

[1]We did not conduct a comprehensive review of all the initiatives we identified in our 2012 report since that was not within the scope of this review. In the process of this review, we did obtain some new information pertaining to selected global and in-region sourcing initiatives, which is reflected in this appendix. However, we did not talk to or obtain information from the government of the DRC on in-region initiatives or legislation related to conflict minerals because this was outside of the scope of our current review.

[2]Organisation for Economic Co-operation and Development, *OECD Due Diligence Guidance for Responsible Supply Chains of Minerals from Conflict-Affected and High-Risk Areas*, second edition (OECD Publishing, 2011). Accessed July 2, 2013, http://dx.doi.org/10.1787/9789264185050-en. The guidance was adopted on May 25, 2011.

and initial impact of due diligence in the tin, tantalum, and tungsten upstream supply chain.[3]

Conflict-Free Smelter Program

The Conflict-Free Smelter Program is a voluntary program in which smelters undergo an independent third party audit, in accordance with the OECD Due Diligence Guidance, to verify the origin of minerals processed at their facilities. The EICC and GeSI have also developed audit protocols for the program in consultation with a number of stakeholders—including NGOs, smelters, component manufacturers, original equipment manufacturers, and industry associations within and outside the electronics industry—to ensure wide-spread support for the program. In December 2010, the first tantalum smelter was certified conflict-free through the program after successfully undergoing an audit, and as of May 1, 2013, 18 of approximately 23 tantalum smelting companies had been certified as conflict-free. As of May 1, 2013, 5 tin smelting companies had been certified as conflict-free, 7 tungsten smelting companies had begun discussions with representatives of the program, and 12 gold refining companies had been certified as conflict-free through the program.

World Gold Council's Conflict-Free Gold Standard and Tools

The World Gold Council developed and issued the Conflict-Free Gold Standard, an industry-led approach to combat the potential misuse of mined gold to fund armed conflict, in October 2012. The standard was developed with council member companies, which constituted the world's leading gold producers, and with extensive input from stakeholders to establish a common approach by which gold producers can assess and provide assurance that their gold has been extracted in a manner that does not cause, support, or benefit unlawful armed conflict or contribute to serious human rights abuses or breaches of international humanitarian law. According to a World Gold Council official, the participating companies' conformance to the Standard will be externally audited and

---

[3]Organisation for Economic Co-operation and Development, *Downstream Implementation of the OECD Due Diligence Guidance for Responsible Supply Chains of Minerals from Conflict-Affected and High-Risk Areas: Final Downstream Report on One-Year Pilot Implementation of the Supplement on Tin, Tantalum, and Tungsten* (OECD: January 2013); and *Upstream Implementation of the OECD Due Diligence Guidance for Responsible Supply Chains of Minerals from Conflict-Affected and High-Risk Areas: Final Report on One-Year Pilot Implementation of the Supplement on Tin, Tantalum, and Tungsten* (OECD: January 2013).

assured and will operationalize the requirements of OECD guidance. The results of the audit using the standard will be recognized across other stakeholder initiatives such as the London Bullion Market Association's Responsible Gold Guidance. The Standard should also support refiners in meeting their due diligence requirements.

In-Region Sourcing Initiatives

Conflict-Free Tin Initiative

The Conflict-Free Tin Initiative (CFTI) is a pilot that was launched in September 2012 and aims to create demand for conflict-free tin from eastern DRC. The traceability and due diligence mechanism through the ITRI Tin Supply Chain Initiative is operated by Pact, an independent NGO, and is operated out of the Kalimbi mine in South Kivu. According to an NGO, the Netherlands Ministry of Foreign Affairs is a neutral broker that brought the partners along the supply chain together, from mine to smelter to end user. The DRC government and local civil society are closely involved in the initiative, which is structured within the framework of the International Conference of the Great Lakes Region (ICGLR) and will be consistent with the due diligence guidance of OECD. CFTI reported that between October 2012 and January 2013, 210 tons of materials were produced in the Kalimbi mine and the first container of conflict-free tin was transported to the trader in the DRC in December 2012. In January 2013, the first two containers of conflict-free tin were shipped to the smelter in Malaysia. The CFTI reports that next steps will involve the conflict-free tin making its way from the smelter to soldering companies and eventually to end users as finished product.

ICGLR's Regional Certification Mechanism and Other Initiatives

The ICGLR started working with an NGO in 2010 to develop a regional certification mechanism to ensure that conflict minerals are fully traceable. ICGLR's regional certification mechanism may enable member countries and their mining companies to demonstrate where and under what conditions minerals were produced; through the regional certification mechanism, individual member governments are to issue ICGLR regional certificates for those mineral shipments that are in compliance with the standards of the mechanism. According to an official at a partnering NGO, the first two certificates out of the region were scheduled to come from sites in Rwanda and DRC in the late spring and from Uganda by December 2013. However, State indicated that the certificates from

Rwanda and DRC have been delayed and will likely not be issued until late summer 2013. Regional certificates from other ICGLR countries will take some time because of capacity issues.

According to USAID, in addition to the regional certification mechanism, ICGLR's other initiatives focused on eliminating the illegal exploitation of natural resources include harmonization of national legislation, formalization of the artisanal mining sector, formalization of the extractives industries transparency initiative, a whistleblowing mechanism, and a regional database on the flow of minerals.

Appendix IV: GAO Contacts and Staff Acknowledgments

GAO Contact	Lawrance L. Evans, Jr., (202) 512-4802 or evansl@gao.gov
Staff Acknowledgments	In addition to the individual named above, Godwin Agbara, Assistant Director; Andrea Riba Miller; Kyerion Printup; Justin Fisher; Debbie Chung; Ernie Jackson; Russ Burnett; Etana Finkler; Brian Hackney; and Leah DeWolf made key contributions to this report.